This book belong

This book is dedicated to my children - Mikey, Kobe, and Jojo.

Paperback ISBN: 978-1-63731-380-0
Hardcover ISBN: 978-1-63731-382-4

Printed and bound in the USA.
NinjaLifeHacks.tv

Ninja Life Hacks®

NINJAS
Go to School

By Mary Nhin

Ninja Life Hacks®

There are so many chances to be kind at school,
Kind Ninja just can't wait.
So they pack their bag, they make their lunch,
And are fast asleep by eight!

Next morning, when Kind Ninja gets to school,
Their friends start to arrive.
They give high fives and start to dance,
It's a ninja high five jive!

Teacher takes all the ninjas inside,
They need to find their seat.
Kind Ninja helps everyone to their place,
And finds new ninjas to meet.

During lessons, Kind Ninja starts their work,
But then they hear a sound,
They rush to pick up pencils and pens,
That others have dropped on the ground.

They go on yard duty to pick up trash,
They comfort kids who are crying.
They push the ninjas on the swing,
So that it feels like flying!

They encourage and run with the runners,
Training for a track meet.
And then, when lunchtime is over,
They collapse into their seat!

When Kind Ninja wakes up, Teacher says,
'You help other ninjas so well.
But it makes you so tired, Kind Ninja,
You slept through the home time bell!'

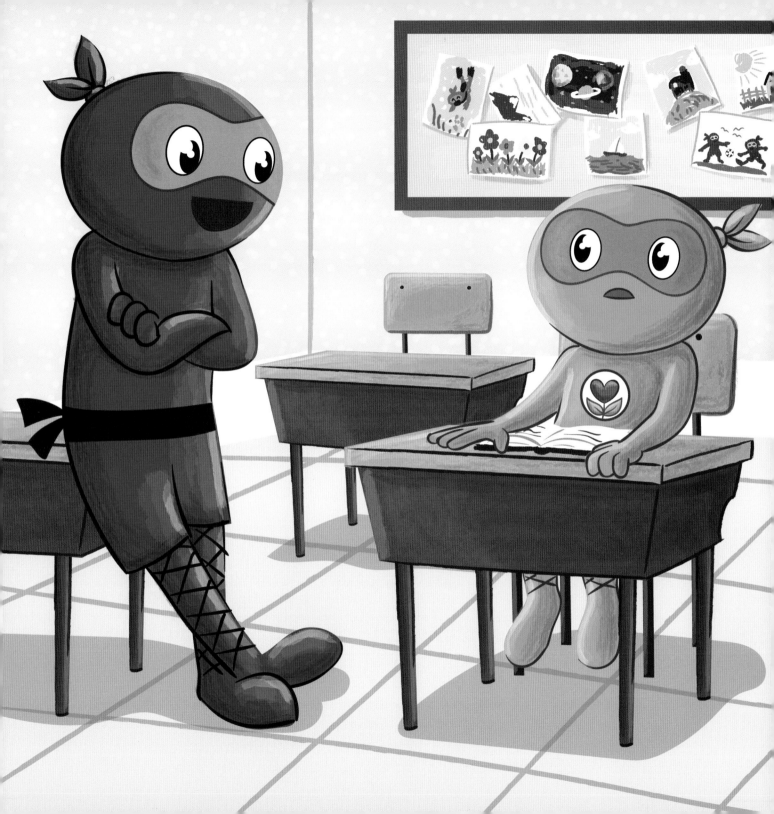

That night, as Kind Ninja lies in bed,
They realize what they must do.
'I'll be kind to others,' they say to themselves,
'But I have to be kind to me, too!'

From that day on, when it comes to kindness,
Kind Ninja still can't be beat.
But now they get all their work done **first**,
And they don't fall asleep in their seat!